SUPERSTARS of PRO FOOTBALL

THE MANNING BROTHERS

Hal Marcovitz

Mason Crest Publishers

Produced by OTTN Publishing in association with
21st Century Publishing and Communications, Inc.

MASON CREST PUBLISHERS INC.
370 Reed Road
Broomall, Pennsylvania 19008
(866) MCP-BOOK (toll free)
www.masoncrest.com

Printed in the United States of America.

First Printing

9 8 7 6 5 4 3 2 1

Library of Congress Cataloging-in-Publication Data

Marcovitz, Hal.
   The Manning brothers / Hal Marcovitz.
      p. cm. — (Superstars of pro football)
   Includes bibliographical references.
   ISBN-13: 978-1-4222-0543-3 (hardcover) — ISBN-10: 1-4222-0543-6 (hardcover)
   ISBN-13: 978-1-4222-0828-1 (pbk.) — ISBN-10: (invalid) 1-4227-0828-1 (pbk.)
   1. Manning, Peyton—Juvenile literature. 2. Manning, Eli, 1981–   —Juvenile
literature. 3. Football players—United States—Biography—Juvenile literature. I. Title.
GV939.A1M367 2008
796.33092'2—dc22
[B]   2008028189

Publisher's note:
All quotations in this book come from original sources, and contain the spelling
and grammatical inconsistencies of the original text.

◀◀ CROSS-CURRENTS ▶▶

In the ebb and flow of the currents of life we are each influenced
by many people, places, and events that we directly experience or
have learned about. Throughout the chapters of this book you will
come across **CROSS-CURRENTS** reference bubbles. These bubbles
direct you to a **CROSS-CURRENTS** section in the back of the
book that contains fascinating and informative sidebars
and related pictures. Go on. ▶▶

◀◀CONTENTS▶▶

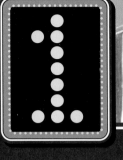

MOST VALUABLE PLAYERS

By January 2007, quarterback Peyton Manning had led the Indianapolis Colts to the playoffs in seven of his nine seasons in the National Football League. But each time, the Colts had fallen short of making it to the Super Bowl. Now, as Peyton glanced at the game clock during the fourth quarter of the **American Football Conference** (AFC) Championship game, it appeared likely the Colts would come up short once again.

With little time left in the game and the Colts down by three points, Peyton faced the task of driving his team the length of

With head coach Tony Dungy at his side, Indianapolis Colts quarterback Peyton Manning holds up the Vince Lombardi Trophy, February 4, 2007. The Lombardi Trophy is awarded to the team that wins the Super Bowl, and Peyton had just led Indianapolis to victory in Super Bowl XLI.

the field to score the go-ahead touchdown against the Colts' long-time rivals, the New England Patriots. If the Colts failed to score, the Patriots would win the AFC title and advance to Super Bowl XLI. Peyton also knew that if he failed to lead a successful drive, he would hear the old criticisms once again—that he could not win the big game.

Rocky Start

Peyton Manning grew up around football. His father, Archie, had been a top college quarterback at the University of Mississippi. Archie Manning played in the NFL during the 1970s and 1980s. Despite possessing great talent, Archie had the misfortune of playing his entire career for some truly abysmal teams. Although he spent 14 seasons in the NFL, he never made it to the playoffs.

Archie did, however, pass his enormous talent on to his sons, Peyton and Eli. Both Manning brothers compiled stellar careers as college quarterbacks and now play in the NFL. Five years younger than Peyton, Eli is the quarterback of the New York Giants. Like Peyton, during his first years in the league Eli was often criticized as a quarterback who could not win the big game.

As Peyton strapped on his helmet late in the AFC Championship game on January 21, 2007, he glanced at the scoreboard clock. Just 2 minutes and 17 seconds remained. To win the game and advance to the Super Bowl, Peyton would have to drive the Colts 80 yards for a touchdown. He started the drive with a quick pass to **wide receiver** Reggie Wayne. Then he hit tight end Bryan Fletcher for a 32-yard gain. Next, he completed another pass to Wayne. A penalty by the Patriots moved the ball to the 11-yard line. Peyton handed off three times to running back Joseph Addai, who finally plunged into the end zone for a TD.

The Patriots got the ball back with just a minute left on the clock. They drove to the Indianapolis 45-yard line before quarterback Tom Brady threw an **interception**. The Colts were headed to the Super Bowl. Said Peyton,

> **"It certainly wasn't the situation you want to be in. We hated to get down like that. Hardly anybody comes back against the Patriots when they have a lead like that. But we relied on our veteran leadership."**

CROSS-CURRENTS

Read "Roman Numerals and the Super Bowl" to learn why the NFL identifies its biggest game using Roman numerals. Go to page 47. ▶▶

Two weeks later the Colts played the Chicago Bears for the Super Bowl XLI trophy. After a rocky start—the Bears jumped out to a 14–6 first-quarter lead—Peyton settled in, quarterbacking an offense that dominated the

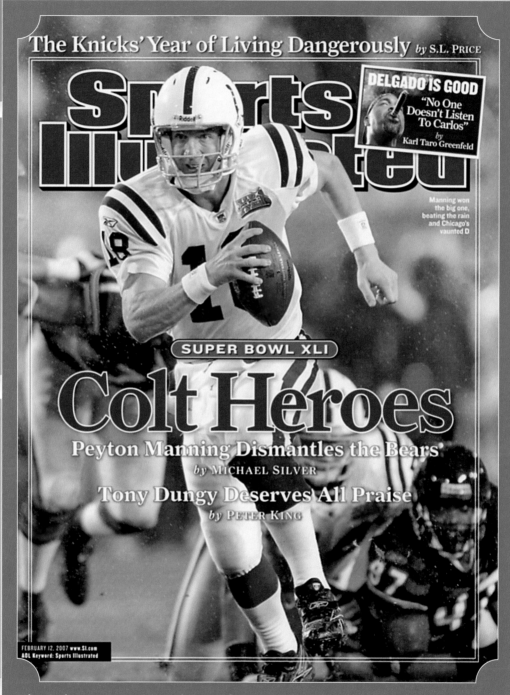

The February 12, 2007, issue of *Sports Illustrated* featured Peyton Manning on the cover. Throwing for 247 yards and a touchdown, Peyton had garnered MVP honors for Super Bowl XLI.

Bears. Playing mostly through a driving rainstorm, Peyton passed for 247 yards, completing 25 of 38 passes in leading the Colts to a 29–17 win. Peyton's solid performance earned him recognition as the game's Most Valuable Player. Finally he had shaken off the reputation as the quarterback who could not win the big game.

Eli Manning and head coach Tom Coughlin celebrate the New York Giants' victory in Super Bowl XLII, February 3, 2008. Like Peyton a year before, Eli was named Super Bowl MVP.

Eluding the Rush

A year later, younger brother Eli also wanted to prove he could win the big game. After an up-and-down season, his Giants team caught fire in the playoffs, upsetting the Green Bay Packers to win the National Football Conference title. Now Eli and the Giants faced the daunting task of defeating the New England Patriots—who had not lost a game all season—in Super Bowl XLII.

With just a little more than two minutes to play in the Super Bowl, the Giants found themselves down by four points. To win the game, Eli would have to guide the offense 83 yards to the New England end zone. Eli started the New York drive by hitting receiver Plaxico Burress with a quick strike. He kept the ball moving, and running back Brandon Jacobs made a key play to pick up a key first **down**. After a sack and a near-interception by the Patriots, Eli dropped back to pass. Three Patriot defenders broke into the pocket, but somehow Eli managed to elude the rush. Scrambling to his right, he saw receiver David Tyree in the middle of the field. He fired the pass to Tyree, who was covered by Patriots defender Rodney Harrison. Both players jumped for the ball. Tyree outwrestled Harrison, making an awkward catch by pinning the ball against his helmet. The circus catch put the Giants in striking distance of the end zone. Moments later, Eli hit Burress for the game-winning score. The Giants' 17–14 win was one of the biggest upsets in Super Bowl history.

For engineering the game-winning drive, Eli received the Most Valuable Player award. The back-to-back Super Bowl MVP wins by the Mannings marked the first time in the history of pro football that brothers have won the honor. After the game Plaxico Burress said of his quarterback,

> **"A lot of people got down on him early in the year, a lot of criticism, but he stayed true to himself. He stayed Eli, kept upbeat, kept his focus, didn't let anybody get in his head and just kept playing."**

CROSS-CURRENTS

To learn about other siblings who have achieved fame in the same fields, read "Successful Siblings." Go to page 47. ▶▶

A FOOTBALL HERITAGE

At Isidore Newman High School in New Orleans, Louisiana, Peyton Manning played quarterback, throwing the ball most often to his favorite receiver—his older brother Cooper. It was 1991, and the "Manning-to-Manning" attack was making headlines across the state. Isidore Newman lost only once during the regular season, and reached the semifinals of the Louisiana high school playoffs. Said Peyton,

"For a quarterback, there's nothing like having your brother as your primary receiver. You're on the same

genetic wavelength. You know each other's every move. And you've been living in the same house together all your lives. How could you beat that?"

Cooper is the oldest of the Manning boys, born in 1974 to Archie and Olivia Manning. Peyton was born in 1976, and Eli followed in 1981. All three boys expected to follow in their father's footsteps, playing football at the University of Mississippi and then going on to the NFL. Cooper graduated from Isidore Newman in 1992 and won a football scholarship to "Ole Miss," but in his freshman year he was diagnosed with a spinal deformity that had been causing numbness in his fingers. The condition was corrected with surgery, but Cooper's football career was over.

University of Southern California quarterback Matt Leinart (second from left) is in good company as he receives the 2004 Manning Trophy, given to the college QB judged best by the Sugar Bowl Committee. Peyton (left), Eli, and Archie Manning were all first-round draft picks in the NFL.

Had Cooper remained with the Mississippi football team, Peyton would have played there as well so that the brothers could continue the Manning-to-Manning attack in college. With no opportunity to play with his brother, Peyton started entertaining the notion of playing college football elsewhere.

CROSS-CURRENTS

For information on the life and career of Peyton and Eli's football-star father, read "Archie Manning." Go to page 48. ▶▶

Recruited by Colleges

As he completed his stellar career at Isidore Newman and prepared to graduate in spring 1994, Peyton found himself the most heavily recruited high school athlete in the country. Sixty major universities offered him **scholarships**. He constantly fielded phone calls and received letters from coaches, asking him to consider their schools. Many coaches visited the Manning home in New Orleans, promising that Peyton would start at quarterback. Peyton later said,

> **❝I loved the recruiting, all of it. I read all the letters, answered all the phone calls. I read the media guides cover to cover. I loved my visits to schools. I loved talking with the coaches who came to visit me. I loved to question them. It was an incredible learning experience.❞**

Finally Peyton visited the University of Tennessee in Knoxville. Oddly, Tennessee was the only place Peyton visited that did not make him feel like a celebrity. Instead he felt very comfortable at Tennessee—as though he would be just another player. When he decided to attend Tennessee, fans of Ole Miss became very angry. Some sent nasty letters or made irate phone calls to the Manning home. But Peyton's parents stood behind their son's decision, and in the fall of 1994 Peyton enrolled as a **freshman** at Tennessee.

Great College Career

The quarterback would go on to compile an impressive career at Tennessee. He helped the Volunteers become a dominant team in the National Collegiate Athletic Association's (NCAA's) Southeastern Conference (SEC). Perhaps his finest game was played near the end of his college career. The Volunteers were ranked third in the country,

Cooper Manning (right) congratulates his brother Eli following the Giants' triumph in Super Bowl XLII. The oldest of the Manning boys, Cooper was himself a standout football player but had to give up the game because of a spinal condition.

and hoped to make a run for the national championship. But to be selected for the Orange Bowl, a major bowl game, the Vols had to win the SEC title against Auburn University.

Tennessee played a sloppy game. The Volunteers had four **fumbles**, and by halftime Auburn held a 20–10 lead. Early in the third quarter, Peyton engineered a scoring drive, closing the gap to 20–17. On the Vols' next possession, Peyton put his team in a position to score again. But his pass to a receiver was bobbled, enabling an Auburn player to pick the ball off and then return the interception deep into Tennessee territory. After that, Auburn's offense scored an easy touchdown to go up by a score of 27–17.

Peyton directed another Tennessee touchdown drive, but the extra point was blocked, and an Auburn player returned the ball

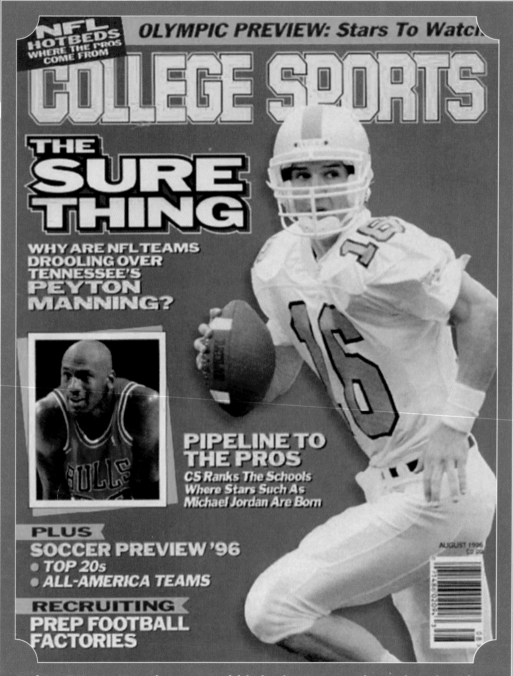

NFL HOTBEDS WHERE THE PROS COME FROM

OLYMPIC PREVIEW: Stars To Watch

COLLEGE SPORTS

THE SURE THING

WHY ARE NFL TEAMS DROOLING OVER TENNESSEE'S PEYTON MANNING?

PIPELINE TO THE PROS
CS Ranks The Schools Where Stars Such As Michael Jordan Are Born

PLUS
SOCCER PREVIEW '96
- TOP 20s
- ALL-AMERICA TEAMS

RECRUITING
PREP FOOTBALL FACTORIES

AUGUST 1996

Before Peyton Manning entered his junior year at the University of Tennessee, NFL scouts already considered him a top prospect, as the August 1996 issue of *College Sports* magazine noted. Peyton would be selected first overall in the 1998 NFL draft.

to the end zone for two points. In the fourth quarter, with his team down 29–23, Peyton hit Tennessee receiver Marcus Nash for a 73-yard touchdown. Tennessee held on to win, 30–29. Peyton threw for 373 yards and four TDs that day. More important, the victory earned Tennessee a berth in the Orange Bowl—and a shot at a national championship.

Tennessee's title dreams would not be fulfilled, however. Facing the University of Nebraska in the Orange Bowl, the Vols were simply overmatched. Peyton didn't play particularly well in his final college game, and Nebraska cruised to a 42–17 victory.

Ready for the NFL

Despite this disappointment, Peyton had done everything that he had been asked to do. His record as a starting quarterback in college had been 39 wins and six losses, and he had been a finalist for the Heisman Trophy—the highest award for college football players—in his sophomore, junior, and senior years. He also set many University of Tennessee passing records, including most career touchdown passes (89). Peyton was regarded as one of the top prospects coming out of college. NFL scouts felt that Peyton's size (he is six feet five inches tall and about 230 pounds) and his maturity would make him an outstanding pro quarterback. In April 1998, the Indianapolis Colts made Peyton the top selection in the **NFL draft**.

A month before the start of the 1998 NFL season, Peyton signed the largest **contract** for a **rookie** in NFL history. The deal included a salary of $1 million per year, plus a signing **bonus** of $11.6 million. Peyton had become rich, but now he would have to prove himself among the pros.

CROSS-CURRENTS

To learn more about the most prestigious award given to a college football player, read "The Heisman Trophy." Go to page 49. ▶▶

GETTING SERIOUS ABOUT FOOTBALL

Peyton and Cooper Manning grew up among pro football players. Their father would often take them to New Orleans Saints practices, where they could watch professionals at work. But Eli was only four years old when Archie Manning retired from football, so he missed out on that experience.

Still, Eli possessed an abundance of talent, which he displayed at Isidore Newman High School. Like Peyton, Eli became the school's starting quarterback as a sophomore. He also played on the school's baseball and basketball teams. By his senior year, Eli was the object of intense recruiting by several major colleges. Finally, he selected Ole Miss.

Eli, the youngest of the Manning brothers, followed in the footsteps of his father by attending the University of Mississippi. During his football career at Ole Miss, Eli would break his father's passing records.

Eli did not immediately establish himself as a star player when he arrived at the school in the fall of 1999. He seemed to lack Peyton's intense desire for competition. Peyton was outgoing and friendly and loved a good joke. Eli was shy and spoke few words. What's more, Peyton loved to study game films and spend hours talking to coaches about strategy, play selection, and other mental aspects of the game. As for Eli, he always did what the coaches asked him to do, but no more. He did not spend hours studying game films but preferred instead to hang out with friends. In high school, his laid-back attitude earned him the nickname "Easy Eli."

During his freshman year at Ole Miss, Eli did not even get on the field. He was "redshirted" by the coach, meaning he attended practices during the week but was not permitted to suit up on game day. For Eli it was a period of uncertainty. Did he really want to play big-time football? In January 2000, a few weeks after the end of his redshirt season, he was arrested by local police outside his fraternity house and charged with public drunkenness. A few days later, the Mississippi coach, David Cutcliffe, called Eli into his office. Said Cutcliffe,

CROSS-CURRENTS

Read "What Is a Redshirt?" to understand how young players learn their positions before appearing in college games. Go to page 50. ▶▶

❝I asked him if he really wanted to be a big-time quarterback, or was he just here to play a little football, have a good time and get through? And I told him to think about it before he answered.❞

Taking Football Seriously

Eli made up his mind to get serious about football. He started spending more time preparing for games, lifting weights, and developing his skills. He started the 2000 season as a backup quarterback, but in the final game of the year, the Music City Bowl against West Virginia, his coach sent him in to play the fourth quarter.

At that point in the game, the Ole Miss Rebels were trailing, 49–16. With no hope of winning, the coach simply wanted to see how Eli handled himself on the field. On a frigid, windy, and icy day, Eli staged an incredible comeback, leading a Rebels offense

Under pressure from the University of Nebraska pass rush, Eli Manning looks downfield for an open receiver during action from the MainStay Independence Bowl, December 27, 2002. Eli led Ole Miss to a 27–23 victory in the game.

that scored 22 unanswered points in the span of less than seven minutes. With just a few minutes left in the game, Eli was leading the Rebels downfield toward another score when he made his only mistake: He threw an interception that snuffed out the rally. He said,

❝Once we got close, I just couldn't finish it off. I wish I could have back that pass that was intercepted.❞

The game may have ended in a 49–38 victory for West Virginia, but it established Eli as the Ole Miss starter for the next season.

The following September, in his first game as the Ole Miss starting quarterback against Murray State, Eli threw 18 straight completions and five touchdown passes to set school records—feats that even the great Archie Manning had never accomplished at Mississippi.

Setting Records

Other spectacular games would follow. In a game against Arkansas later that season, Eli threw for 312 yards and six touchdowns in a 58–56 overtime loss to the Razorbacks. Even though the Rebels lost the game, fans were stunned by Eli's performance on the field.

Eli Manning (left) and his Ole Miss teammates practice for their January 2, 2004, meeting with Oklahoma State in the Cotton Bowl. In that game—his last as a college player—Eli threw for two touchdowns and ran for a third. Ole Miss won, 31–28.

By his senior season, 2003, Eli and the Rebels were in position to contend for a Southeastern Conference title. Across the SEC, other coaches were in awe of Eli's talent. Said Auburn coach Tommy Tuberville,

"They don't come much better than him, and I've been in this business a long time. He has really shown improvement each week over the past four years."

Mississippi would fall short of winning the SEC title—Louisiana State University captured the championship that year. Nevertheless, the Rebels received an invitation to compete in the Cotton Bowl in January 2004. In Eli's final game as a Rebel, he led Ole Miss to a 31–28 victory over Oklahoma State. He threw for 259 yards and two touchdowns and pushed his way over the goal line on a quarterback keeper to score another touchdown. That score came in the fourth quarter to seal the win for the Rebels. It capped a 13-play, 97-yard drive that included two clutch passes by Eli on third-and-long plays. After the game, Eli said,

"Everything about this year has been great. It's been a great run. . . . It's been a fun ride. It has to end sometime. We picked a great way to end it."

The victory over Oklahoma State marked the first time Ole Miss had won a major college bowl since Archie Manning led the Rebels to victory in the 1970 Sugar Bowl. In leading the Mississippi offense for three seasons, Eli broke his father's passing records at Ole Miss, setting his own school record with 10,119 passing yards.

As Eli was setting those records, NFL scouts had been watching his progress. In April 2004 the San Diego Chargers made him the top selection in the NFL draft. Moments after NFL commissioner Paul Tagliabue called Eli's name, the Chargers engineered a trade that sent him to the New York Giants. Before reporting to training camp that summer, Eli signed a contract with the Giants for $54 million over six years.

CROSS-CURRENTS
Read "The NFL Draft" to find out more about the way college players are selected by professional teams. Go to page 50. ▶▶

Tough Lessons

While Eli was lighting up scoreboards in the Southeastern Conference, his older brother was finding out just how difficult it can be to succeed as an NFL quarterback. Peyton's first season as a professional was filled with frustrations. The rookie started all 16 games, but his team was awful. The Colts stumbled to a 3–13 record. The experience of playing for a losing team came as something of a shock to Peyton. During eight years of playing high school and college football, Peyton had lost a *total* of 11 games.

The 10th loss of Peyton's rookie season was particularly painful. Playing the Baltimore Ravens, Peyton managed to keep the score close. With less than two minutes left on the clock, he was driving the Colts down the field for a touchdown that would have tied the game. With the Colts in scoring position, Peyton eluded the Ravens' rush, hitting running back Marshall Faulk with a quick pass. But Faulk bobbled the ball, and a Baltimore defender stepped in to intercept the pass. Final score: Ravens 38, Colts 31.

Despite the Colts' dismal record, there were indications that the team was gelling behind its young quarterback. Peyton was proving to be both a quick learner and a good leader. Always an avid student of the game, Peyton spent hours each week studying the opposing teams' defenses on film. He became a master of reading defensive formations during the game, anticipating the schemes his opponents planned to throw at him. He also mastered the Colts' playbook and was able to easily change plays at the line after glancing at the opposing defensive formation. After the Ravens game, Ravens **cornerback** Rod Woodson said,

> **"**He's got good poise, great poise for a rookie. Sometimes he gets a little impatient, but take your hat off to him. He's not making a lot of mistakes.**"**

Record Bonus

The Colts' patience with Peyton paid off in 1999. In his second season, Peyton threw for 4,135 yards and led the team to a 13–3 record and a division title. In January 2000, the Colts prepared to play the Tennessee Titans in the playoffs in Peyton's first professional postseason game. For the quarterback, the game carried some extra motivation. It would be played in Tennessee, in front of fans who had supported him during his four years of college.

For Peyton, though, the game did not go well. The Titans played an aggressive defense, roughing up Peyton and preventing his speedy receivers from getting open downfield. Titans running back Eddie George dominated the Colts' defense, gaining 162 rushing yards. The game ended in a 19–16 Titans victory. Said Colts coach Jim Mora,

❝We had a hard time coming up with anything big or getting any big chunks of yardage. We have a very, very young offense that is not near what it is going to be at some point. Sometimes, you do things and expect it to happen every game. Today, we just got outplayed by a better football team.❞

Peyton Manning lines up over center Jeff Saturday to take a snap. From early on in his pro career, Peyton—a tireless student of the game—was adept at reading NFL defenses and changing offensive plays at the line of scrimmage.

With his offensive line providing excellent protection, Peyton Manning unleashes a pass against the Houston Texans, November 14, 2004. Peyton threw 5 touchdown passes in the game, a 49–14 Indianapolis victory, en route to a record-setting 49 TDs during the 2004 season.

That first playoff loss against the Tennessee Titans in 2000 marked the beginning of a postseason jinx that would follow Peyton and the Colts for seven years, until they were finally able to win Super Bowl XLI. Still, under Peyton, the Colts developed into one of the best offenses in the league. Throughout that period, the Colts suffered just one losing season (in 2001). In 2004, 2005, and 2006, Peyton's quarterback rating—the complicated statistical formula that gauges a quarterback's performance—was highest in the league. He led the league in passing in 2000 and 2003 and was voted into the Pro Bowl—the NFL's all-star game—eight times. In 2003 and 2004, he was named league MVP.

In March 2004, the Colts made a long-term commitment to Peyton, negotiating a new contract that paid him $98 million over seven years. The contract included a $34.5 million signing bonus—the largest signing bonus awarded to a player in NFL history. Peyton admitted to being awed by the size of the contract offered to him by the Colts. He said,

CROSS-CURRENTS

For information about another Colts quarterback who is considered one of the all-time greats, read "Johnny U." Go to page 51. ▶▶

"Everybody's happy, and like I said, I'm just relieved it's over with. I'm looking forward to the 2004 season and look forward to winning next season."

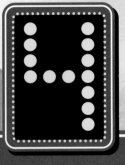

THE MANNING BOWL

Week 1 of the 2006 NFL season would see history made. On the evening of September 10, on national television, the Indianapolis Colts, quarterbacked by Peyton Manning, were scheduled to meet the New York Giants, quarterbacked by Eli Manning, in a game the press dubbed the "Manning Bowl." Brothers had never started an NFL game as opposing quarterbacks.

The game would also make history within the Manning family. Growing up in New Orleans, Peyton and Eli had never really competed against one another. Because Peyton is five years

Peyton and Eli Manning chat on the field at Giants Stadium in East Rutherford, New Jersey, several hours before their much-anticipated season opener, September 10, 2006. For the first time in NFL history, two brothers would be the starting quarterbacks of opposing teams.

older than Eli, the two rarely played against one another. According to Peyton, their competition had been limited to some friendly games of basketball in the driveway in which Peyton would agree not to block more than two of Eli's shots per game.

In fact it was much more common for Peyton to beat up his younger brother, as older brothers are often prone to do. Recalled Eli,

> **"Peyton tortured me pretty good. He would pin me down and knock on my chest with his knuckles and make me name ten schools in the SEC. . . . He wouldn't stop until I did. I probably wouldn't know all my divisions and teams if it wasn't for that."**

CROSS-CURRENTS

Check out "When Siblings Compete" to learn about some other siblings who have faced each other in high-profile athletic competitions. Go to page 52.

Lacking Consistency

The hype for the game started months in advance. Over the summer, reporters interviewed Cooper, Archie, and Olivia Manning to find out which team the family would be rooting for. Members of the Manning family remained steadfastly neutral. Shortly before the game, Archie said,

> **"I love both my sons equally. If it was the end of the season and one of the teams needed a win to make the playoffs, I might root for that team. But this is early in the season."**

The game was scheduled for Giants Stadium in East Rutherford, New Jersey. It meant that Eli would be playing in front of the hometown fans, which is often an advantage because loud and enthusiastic fans can distract the visitors. Still, the Colts were favored to win. Eli was starting his third year in the league. During 2004, his rookie year in the NFL, he had spent the first half of the season on the bench, playing behind starter Kurt Warner. Giants coach Tom Coughlin did not insert Eli as starter until the 10th game of the season. Eli played inconsistently, making some rookie mistakes. However, in the final game of the year, he engineered a dramatic, come-from-behind win over the Dallas Cowboys.

For the first half of the 2005 season, Eli's play had again been inconsistent, although in the second half of the year he turned in some solid performances in leading the Giants to an 11–5 record and a berth in the postseason. (They lost their playoff game to the Carolina Panthers by a 23–0 score.) Eli's challenge in 2006 was to show consistency and lead his talented team deep into the playoffs.

Meanwhile, Peyton had blossomed into a veteran quarterback at the helm of a team that had visited the postseason many times. By 2006, many football experts believed the Colts were poised to make a run at the Super Bowl. Before the first **kickoff** on Week 1 of the season, most football experts were picking the Colts to win their matchup against the Giants.

CROSS-CURRENTS

For the history of the stadium where Eli's team plays its home games, read "Giants Stadium." Go to page 53. ▶▶

Eli Manning throws a pass during the Giants' 31–7 loss to the Washington Redskins at FedEx Field in Landover, Maryland, December 5, 2004. Eli played inconsistently in his rookie year, finishing the season with six touchdown passes and nine interceptions.

The Giants' offense lines up against the Colts' defense in action from Week 1 of the 2006 season. In the game, Eli Manning held his own against his more highly touted brother, throwing for 247 yards and two touchdowns to Peyton's 276 yards and one TD.

Turning Point

Peyton started off in top form, firing passes on four of the first five plays. He marched the Colts down the field in a methodical 17-play drive that burned more than nine minutes off the clock. Under Peyton, the Colts were known as a big-play offense. The Giants had to be wary of Colts receivers Marvin Harrison and Reggie Wayne, who could score with a Manning pass from anywhere on the field. For much of the first half, though, Peyton played a much different type of game: He picked apart the Giants' defense with short passes, confusing the Giants with clutch plays when he needed them. Eleven times during the first half, the Colts faced third down. Much to the Giants' frustration, Peyton converted on nine of them.

Before the game, Coach Coughlin decided that he didn't want to put a heavy burden on Eli to carry the offense. Still concerned about Eli's inconsistent play, the coach put the responsibility instead on the Giants' Pro Bowl running back, Tiki Barber. Tiki would finish the game with 18 carries for 110 yards. To keep the Colts' defense guessing, though, Coughlin directed Eli to sprinkle in short passes.

By the end of the first half, the Giants trailed 16–7. The team's lone score came on a second-quarter pass from Eli to receiver Plaxico Burress. Eli had driven the team into scoring position, then lofted a pass into the end zone. Plaxico and a Colts defender both jumped for the ball. Plaxico jumped higher; as the ball bobbled between the two defenders, he pulled in the pass. The play marked a turning point in the game—it gave the Giants confidence that they could play competitively with the Colts.

The Giants took the second-half kickoff and marched down the field against the Colts' defense, putting together an 11-play drive that ended in a 17-yard touchdown pass from Eli to tight end Jeremy Shockey. On the Colts' next possession, the crowd exploded when Peyton threw an interception. With their team just two points down and in scoring position, the fans anticipated a go-ahead score. On the second play of the drive, though, Eli and Tiki botched a handoff. Tiki fumbled, and the Colts recovered the ball. The Colts' offense took the field, and Peyton directed a scoring drive that ended with a one-yard plunge over the goal line by running back Dominic Rhodes.

With the score 23–14, the Giants took the kickoff and put together another impressive drive. Eli spread the ball around, handing off to Tiki and running back Brandon Jacobs. He also passed effectively. After 11 plays, the Giants scored again to tighten the score to 23–21.

The Giants took possession again with less than five minutes to play, deep in their own territory. After completing a pass that gained eight yards, Eli hit receiver Tim Carter with a 19-yard strike. But the referee called Carter with a penalty for pass interference, ruling that the receiver had pushed the defender out of the way to catch the ball. Now backed up deep in their own territory, the Giants faced a third down with 11 yards to go for the first. Eli took the snap and lofted a pass over the middle of the field. It was a poor throw and easily intercepted by a Colts defender. With possession of the ball, the Colts burned off the final moments of the game, kicked a field goal, and won 26–21. Later Eli said,

❝I'm disappointed. That was a game we maybe let slip away.❞

Seconds after the whistle, Eli and Peyton met at midfield to shake hands and exchange words. Even though the brothers were surrounded by a swarm of reporters and cameras, no one but the brothers heard the words they spoke to each other. Afterward, when the Colts quarterback was asked what he said to Eli, Peyton said he told him that he loved him.

Erratic Performances

As far as the statistics were concerned, Eli had held his own. Peyton connected on 25 of 41 passes for 276 yards with a touchdown and an interception, while Eli's statistics included 20 completions in 34 attempts, 247 yards, two touchdowns, and an interception.

Archie knew how devastating it had been to Eli to throw the interception in the closing moments of the game. Archie and Olivia attended the game, then spent time with their sons separately afterward. (Because the Colts had to catch a plane back to Indianapolis, Peyton was unable to make time after the game to spend with his younger brother.) Still, Archie did speak with Eli after the game and knew how much it troubled him to lose. He said,

"Oh my God, I hurt for him. I know what it feels like. Eli was hurting. I mean, I know him. It killed him. I could tell. He was hurting. He really was."

Eli followed up the loss to the Colts with a solid performance against the Philadelphia Eagles. He threw for a career-high 371 yards in rallying the Giants from a 24–7 fourth-quarter deficit to an overtime win. By midseason, the Giants had compiled a 6–2 record and seemed to be in control of their division. During the second half of

From the expressions on the Manning brothers' faces after the 2006 season opener, it would be difficult to tell whose team had won and whose had lost. Peyton's Colts had triumphed, 26–21.

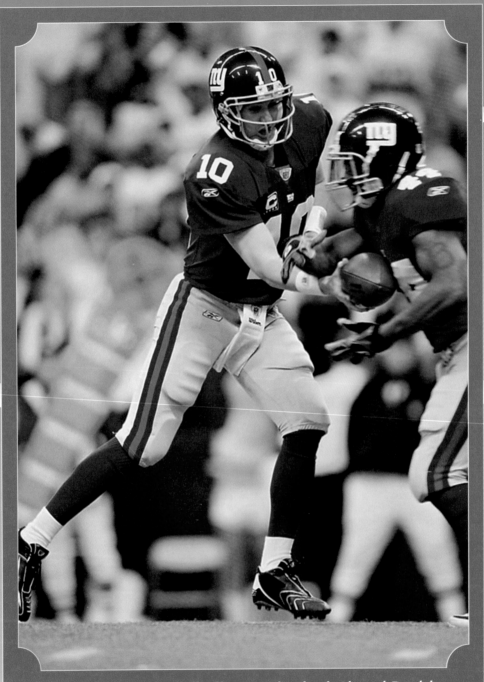

Eli Manning hands the ball off to running back Ahmad Bradshaw in action from the 2007 season. After New York's disappointing 8–8 finish in 2006, there was a lot of pressure on Eli, head coach Tom Coughlin, and the rest of the team to win in 2007.

the season, though, the Giants suffered through some key injuries. Eli played inconsistently—in a loss to the Chicago Bears, he passed for only 141 yards and threw two key interceptions. Later, in a game against the Saints, he again threw two costly picks and compiled just 73 yards in total passing. What's more, Tiki Barber's premature announcement that he planned to retire at the end of the season seemed to cause additional turmoil in the Giants' locker room. Coughlin's coaching job was rumored to be on the line. The Giants ended the season at 8–8. They just barely qualified for the playoffs, then lost in the first round to the Philadelphia Eagles.

Of course the Colts would go on to accomplish much more during the 2006 season. Even though the team's defense played poorly at times, Peyton's leadership on offense helped carry the team into the playoffs. Peyton passed for nearly 4,400 yards in leading the Colts to 12 wins. He reserved his best games for the playoffs, rallying the team from behind to beat the rival New England Patriots and then dominating the Bears in the Super Bowl.

For Peyton, the Super Bowl victory was sweet vindication. For years, despite the records he set on the field, he had been criticized as unable to win the big game. Now, the Colts were champions, and Peyton had been named the game's Most Valuable Player.

For Eli, the Giants' playoff loss was the end of a long season. People were saying that he would never be as good as his older brother. But in the next year, Eli would have his own opportunity to silence the critics.

LONG CAREERS AHEAD

E li Manning's 2007 season almost ended during the first game of the year. Playing against the Dallas Cowboys, Eli completed 28 of 41 passes for more than 300 yards and four touchdowns, although the Giants eventually lost the game. Late in the game, he was **sacked** hard by Cowboys linebacker Anthony Spencer, suffering an injury to his right shoulder.

At first the injury didn't seem serious. After picking himself up off the turf, Eli went to the sidelines and threw some passes. He said,

"I threw it, threw it hard, it came out a spiral, and I said, 'All right, I'm going back in.'"

Dallas Cowboys linebacker Anthony Spencer sacks Eli Manning, September 9, 2007. On the play, Eli suffered a severe shoulder sprain. Although Giants team doctors predicted that he might miss a month because of the injury, Eli started the next game.

On the next play, a Giants defender intercepted a pass from Cowboys quarterback Tony Romo. Eli trotted back onto the turf at Texas Stadium and led the team down the field, completing four sharp passes, including a touchdown strike to Plaxico Burress.

During the Cowboys' next possession, though, Eli could feel the pain setting in. When the Giants got the ball back, coach Tom Coughlin sent Eli's backup, Jared Lorenzen, in to finish the game.

The next morning Eli woke up to intense pain in his shoulder. He was unable to throw a football. Two days after the game, Eli sat out practice. Since his days starting at quarterback for Isidore Newman High School, Eli had never missed a game because of an injury—a string that included 41 consecutive starts at quarterback for the Giants. As he endured the soreness in his right shoulder, it seemed that string would soon come to an end.

Catching Fire

Eli was diagnosed with a severe sprain: The ligaments—the tissue connecting the bones in his shoulder—had been overstretched when Anthony tackled him. There is no treatment for sprains other than to let the ligaments heal themselves. At first team doctors predicted it could be a month or more before Eli could play again. By the end of the week, though, Eli found that the pain had subsided. He practiced with the team on Friday and told Coach Coughlin he was ready to play that Sunday against the Green Bay Packers.

Eli played most of that game. By the fourth quarter, the Packers held a 21–13 lead. With about five minutes left to play, Eli threw a pass that was picked off by Packers lineman Corey Williams. Responding to instinct, Eli tried to tackle the massive lineman. Fearing that Eli would aggravate his shoulder, Coughlin pulled him out of the game and sent Lorenzen onto the field. But on his first play, the backup twisted his ankle and hobbled off. Third-string quarterback Anthony Wright finished the game, which ended in a Giants loss.

The Giants were now 0–2 for the season, with their starting quarterback nursing a sore shoulder. What's more, the rest of the team was hardly playing up to its potential. Early in the season Giants owner John Mara questioned Eli's ability to lead the team. He said,

Eli scrambles to escape the grasp of Green Bay Packers defensive end Cullen Jenkins, September 16, 2007. The Packers won the game, 35–13, dropping New York's record to 0–2.

❝The only thing we evaluate is 'Can we win with this guy?' That's the one thing. When we talk about any player at the end of the season, the No.1 question is 'Will he help us win?' And to take it one step further, 'Can we win a championship with this guy?'**❞**

The words seemed to spark Eli as well as the other Giants players. After the Packers loss, the Giants put together a six-game winning

With his line taking care of the New England pass rush, Peyton Manning looks downfield for an open receiver. When the Colts and Patriots met on September 4, 2007, both clubs boasted a 7–0 record. The Patriots won the battle of the undefeated teams, 24–21.

streak. The team finished the year at 10–6, making the playoffs and eventually winning the Super Bowl.

Playing with Momentum

While the Giants stumbled at the start of their season, the Colts entered the 2007 season with momentum, capturing their first seven games. It seemed as though Peyton would lead his team to a second Super Bowl appearance, but as the Colts defeated opponent after opponent, another team was having an equally good season. The New England Patriots were matching the Colts win for win. By midseason, both teams were unbeaten—a situation that was destined to change in November when the teams were slated to meet in Indianapolis.

The game had been the subject of intense hype for weeks. Never before had two undefeated teams met so late in the season. On November 4, a national television audience tuned in to watch this battle of unbeaten teams.

For much of the game, the Colts seemed to be in control. Early in the fourth quarter, Peyton scored on a quarterback sneak to give the Colts a lead of 20–10. On the next possession, however, Patriots quarterback Tom Brady hit wide receiver Randy Moss with a 55-yard pass that ended three yards short of a score. On the next play, Brady connected with receiver Wes Welker for a scoring pass.

After the kickoff, Peyton led a drive downfield but the Patriots' rush forced a fumble, which the Colts recovered. Still, the fumble killed the drive, and the Colts were forced to punt. On the Patriots' next possession, Brady hit running back Kevin Faulk with a touch-down pass, putting the Patriots ahead with less than four minutes to play. On the Colts' next series, Patriots lineman Jarvis Green broke through the line, sacked Peyton, and forced another fumble. The Patriots recovered the ball, killed the clock, and claimed the win.

Peyton had trouble shaking off the loss. A week later he played miserably in a Colts loss to the San Diego Chargers, throwing six interceptions. Despite his poor play, he still managed to score three touchdowns late in the game, but the rally fell short and the Colts lost by two points. Peyton recovered a week later, beating the Kansas City Chiefs to notch his 100th career victory as a starting quarter-back. What's more, during the Chiefs game he passed the milestone of 40,000 career passing yards.

The Colts played well for the rest of the season, finishing the year with a 13–3 mark. They lost in the second round of the playoffs, however, losing to the Chargers, 28–24. After the game Peyton said the loss was particularly frustrating because he believed the Colts had the talent to repeat as Super Bowl champions. He said,

> **"What happened last year doesn't make it any easier this year. When you come back and commit yourself to the '07 season and you don't finish it like you want to, it hurts."**

On the same weekend that the Colts fell to the Chargers, Eli and the Giants upset the Dallas Cowboys to advance into the next round of the playoffs. **Sportswriters** could not help but point out that the younger Manning was still in contention for the Super Bowl while the older Manning was not.

Dominating Their Sport

The Mannings are dedicated to football, but they are also dedicated to the community. Away from the field, both Mannings are very involved in charitable work. The brothers participate in an annual football camp headed by their dad at Nicholls State University in Thibodaux, Louisiana, near New Orleans. Each summer about 1,000 high school quarterbacks, receivers, and running backs gather at the Manning Passing Academy to learn the intricacies of the passing game from three of the sport's outstanding quarterbacks.

Most of the players come to the camp from high schools in Louisiana, Mississippi, and other states in the South. Following the devastation to the region caused by Hurricane Katrina in the summer of 2005, the camp took on a special meaning for many of those students, who had been displaced from their homes. In the summer of 2006, Archie, Peyton, and Eli aimed to make the camp the most successful ever so that the displaced players could forget about their troubles for a few days and concentrate on football. Said Eli,

CROSS-CURRENTS

For more information on Peyton and Eli's charitable work, check out "The Mannings and Hurricane Katrina Relief." Go to page 53.

"This is where we grew up, so I always enjoy coming back. It's a tough situation and I'm supportive of New Orleans. A lot of things need to be done, but I have faith."

Meanwhile, back in Indianapolis, Peyton has established the Peyback Foundation, which has supported a number of charities in

Peyton, Archie, and Eli Manning sport milk mustaches in a commercial for the "Got Milk?" ad campaign. The Mannings are also extensively involved in charitable work.

Indiana, including St. Vincent's Children's Hospital in Indianapolis. Since arriving in the city, Peyton has donated so much time and money to the hospital that in 2007 the hospital changed its name to Peyton Manning's Children's Hospital at St. Vincent. Said Vincent C. Caponi, chief executive officer of the hospital,

> **"He is not only an extraordinary football athlete, but also a role model who is committed to giving back to children and the community. Peyton Manning Children's Hospital will complement the high quality of pediatric care that is provided to all patients and families throughout Indiana."**

Eli has also made a commitment to community health care by heading a $2.5 million drive to build the Eli Manning Children's Clinics at the University of Mississippi Medical Center.

Off the field the Mannings stay out of the tabloids. Peyton married his wife Ashley, his former college girlfriend, in 2001. Together Peyton and Ashley have organized Peyton's Pals, a group of volunteers that organizes activities for special-needs children as well as children from neglected and abused backgrounds. In 2006 Peyton, Ashley, and other volunteers organized a four-day cruise to Walt Disney World in Florida for 17 children. Said Ashley,

> **"This was the second year we've done it. A lot of them had never been on a plane let alone on a cruise. I would think it was probably their first time out of Indiana. Just to see the joy on their faces, you can't imagine it. They had probably ten smoothies a day each because it was all you can eat."**

Eli also keeps a low profile off the field. In 2008 he and his girlfriend, fashion designer Abby McGrew, were married.

With Peyton at the peak of his career, and Eli approaching his brother's status as one of the league's top quarterbacks, it appears as though the Mannings will continue dominating their sport for years to come. Said Archie Manning,

Peyton Manning and his wife, Ashley, photographed in 2007. The two, who were college sweethearts, married on March 17, 2001. Ashley Manning, like her husband, devotes considerable time to charity.

Eli Manning and his wife, Abby McGrew. They two met while they were both students at the University of Mississippi. They were married at a private resort in Mexico in April 2008.

"People ask me if I knew this would happen. Or any of it would. If in my wildest dreams I thought that Peyton would be so good, and that right on his heels would come his little brother with similarly developing skills and credentials. The short answer would be, 'Of course not.' As proud as I am, I didn't know. And wouldn't have dared to dream it."

Roman Numerals and the Super Bowl

Why does the National Football League use Roman numerals to designate the Super Bowl?

The custom started in 1972 as the NFL prepared to stage the fifth Super Bowl. **Commissioner** Pete Rozelle thought the use of Roman numerals would give the game a degree of pizzazz. Also, NFL officials wanted to avoid the confusion that had surrounded the game. Since the NFL plays its games in the fall and winter, the Super Bowl is always played in the year following the year in which the regular season is played. Therefore the 2009 Super Bowl pits the conference champions from the 2008 season.

Over the years NFL officials have resisted many calls to drop the Roman numerals, since most people don't understand them and have a hard time matching the symbols with numbers. The NFL likes the elegant status that Roman numerals seem to add to the game. According to Clifford Ando, a professor of Roman literature at the University of Chicago:

❝I suppose Roman numerals have a certain grandeur to them. Both because they're foreign and they're associated with an ancient empire.**❞**

(Go back to page 6.) ◀◀

Successful Siblings

Successful brothers and sisters often achieve fame together—the Brothers Grimm, the Wright Brothers, and the Marx Brothers are examples. But it is far less common for brothers or sisters to reach the top by taking independent paths. Here are some of the brothers and sisters who have excelled on their own in the same fields:

Actor Casey Affleck was nominated for an Academy Award in 2008 as best supporting actor for his role as the man who shot outlaw Jesse James. Ben Affleck, his older brother, is an actor, director, and screenwriter. He won the 1998 Academy Award for writing the screenplay for the film *Good Will Hunting*.

Sisters Charlotte, Emily, and Anne Brontë all contributed important works to British literature. Charlotte is the author of *Jane Eyre*, Emily wrote *Wuthering Heights*, and Anne contributed *Agnes Grey*.

Before becoming the country's 43rd president, George W. Bush served as governor of Texas. His brother, Jeb Bush, is a former governor of Florida. Another powerful family in American politics is the Kennedys. President John F. Kennedy was the nation's 35th chief executive, while his younger brothers Robert and Edward both served in the U.S. Senate.

Bernard J. Shapiro served as president of McGill University in Montreal, Quebec. His brother, Harold T. Shapiro, has served as president of the University of Michigan and Princeton University in New Jersey. (Go back to page 9.) ◀◀

Archie Manning

Archie Manning, the father of Peyton and Eli Manning, remains a very popular and admired figure in New Orleans, in his hometown of Drew, Mississippi, and at the University of Mississippi in Oxford, where he played college football. He is regarded as the greatest athlete to have ever played at Ole Miss; the passing records he set during his college career at Ole Miss stood for many years—until they were broken by his son Eli.

Archie graduated from Ole Miss in 1971 and was selected as the second overall pick in the NFL draft by the New Orleans Saints. After joining the Saints, he embarked on a long and frustrating career as an NFL quarterback. Although he was regarded as a top NFL passer, the Saints and other teams he played for (the Houston Oilers in 1982–83 and the Minnesota Vikings in 1983–84) never surrounded him with top talent. During his 14 years in the NFL, Archie's teams compiled a woeful 35–101–3 record. This is the worst record ever compiled by a quarterback who started more than 100 games.

Despite playing for some truly bad teams, Archie was a pretty good quarterback. In 1978, he was named NFC Player of the Year, and he was chosen for the Pro Bowl, the NFL's annual all-star game, in 1978 and 1979. For his career, he completed more than 55 percent of his passes for 23,911 yards and 125 touchdowns. Archie has never harbored regrets about his career. He said,

> ❝When I finally left the Vikings, it was an upper instead of a downer, a plus instead of a minus. Good-bye football, hello rest of my life. And hello Cooper, Peyton, and Eli, and the football I would enjoy through them. A whole new world.❞

Archie met his wife, Olivia, while in college; she was also attending Ole Miss, and was the school's homecoming queen in her senior year. After retiring from pro football, he worked as a television and radio broadcaster for both college and Saints football games. Archie and his wife have been involved in numerous charitable activities, and in 2007 the Boy Scouts of America awarded him the Silver Buffalo Award, one of Scouting's highest honors, which is given for service to young people. (Go back to page 12.) ◀◀

The Heisman Trophy

The Heisman Trophy is given to the country's best college football player each year. It is generally considered the most prestigious award a college football player can receive.

The award is presented each December, after the regular college games have ended but before the major bowl games. Any college football player is eligible, but the winners usually come from the high-profile NCAA Division I schools that compete for the national championship and play in the major bowls. Sportswriters from all over the country, along with former winners of the award, each get to vote. In addition, there is a fan vote that is taken into account. Voters select three players, with three points awarded to the top choice, two for second, and one for third. The player with the most points is the Heisman winner.

As a sophomore in 1995, Peyton Manning finished sixth in the Heisman Trophy voting, and in his junior season, he finished eighth. Many people expected that he would win the Heisman as a senior, but he finished second in the 1997 balloting to Charles Woodson, a cornerback from Michigan. Woodson was the first defensive player to win the award. Archie Manning later said that there had been too much pressure on Peyton to put up big statistics each week and catch the attention of Heisman voters. (Go back to page 15.)

The Heisman Trophy is given each year to the best college football player in the nation, as voted on by sportswriters and former Heisman winners. In most years, the award goes to a quarterback or a running back.

What Is a Redshirt?

Although Eli Manning joined the University of Mississippi football team in the fall of 1999, he didn't see playing time until the 2000 season. During his freshman year Eli was "redshirted," and therefore not permitted to play.

Under NCAA rules, all student-athletes are limited to four years of competition. Even if a student participates in a single play all season, it still counts as an entire season's eligibility. A redshirted athlete can attend training sessions and practice with the team, although he is not permitted to play in games. For a sport like football, this gives a young player time to learn the complexities of his position, without having to sacrifice a year of eligibility.

A coach will usually redshirt a student if the team has an abundance of players at a particular position competing for playing time. In Eli's case, he was not expected to start, or even play much, as a freshman. Redshirting Eli for the 1999 season meant that he could eventually play four full seasons with the team.

The origin of the term is unclear, but athletic folklore suggests that when the policy was first enacted, coaches made ineligible athletes wear red shirts during the games so that they knew not to send them onto the field during the heat of competition. (Go back to page 18.) ◀◀

The NFL Draft

Eli and Peyton Manning were each the top overall selection in the NFL draft—Peyton in 1998 and Eli in 2004. The draft has been staged annually since 1936 under a concept devised by the league to help weaker teams remain competitive by giving them the rights to sign the best college athletes. Under the rules, the team with the worst record from the previous season picks first, followed next by the team with the second-worst record, and so on until every team makes a pick. Then the process starts again for a second round and continues through seven rounds.

Just because a player goes high in the draft does not guarantee success in the NFL—particularly when it comes to playing quarterback. In 1998 the player taken directly after Peyton Manning was quarterback Ryan Leaf, who went on to have a brief and undistinguished career in the pros. In 1999 quarterback Tim Couch was selected first overall by the Cleveland Browns; he never emerged as a top passer. The player selected directly after Couch, quarterback Donovan McNabb, has blossomed into a perennial all-star for the Philadelphia Eagles. Meanwhile, in the 2000 draft, quarterback Tom Brady was the 199th pick, selected in the sixth round by the New England Patriots. Brady has turned into one of the game's top stars. (Go back to page 21.) ◀◀

"Johnny U"

Peyton Manning may have chalked up some tremendous achievements as quarterback of the Indianapolis Colts, but some football fans do not regard him as the greatest Colts quarterback ever—at least not yet. In the minds of many fans, that status still belongs to Johnny Unitas.

Born in 1933 and raised in Pittsburgh, Johnny played quarterback for his high school team and accepted a scholarship to the University of Louisville, becoming a starter in his freshman year. He was drafted in a late round by the Pittsburgh Steelers in 1955, but was soon released. After a year working in a construction job and making $6 per game playing for a semipro team, Johnny was offered a contract by the Colts—who were playing in Baltimore at the time.

He went on to enjoy an 18-year pro career in which he threw for more than 40,000 yards and 290 touchdowns. His record of throwing touchdown passes in 47 consecutive games still stands.

In 1958, "Johnny U" quarterbacked the Colts to the NFL title, defeating the New York Giants in a nail-biting sudden-death overtime victory that was regarded as the greatest NFL game ever played. Sports experts suggest the game marked the beginning of pro football's rise as the preeminent sport in the United States.

Johnny suffered a fatal heart attack in 2002 while exercising at a gym. (Go back to page 25.)

Saturday Evening Post · December 12, 1964 · 25c

POST

WHAT WILL L.B.J. DO NOW?

A PILGRIMAGE THROUGH THE HAUNTED BATTLEFIELDS OF WORLD WAR II

$1,000,000 TREASURE FIND

Johnny Unitas of the Colts

SOCIETY'S BEST-KEPT SECRET · DO WOMEN RUN THE U.S?

Johnny Unitas, seen here on the cover of the December 12, 1964, issue of The Saturday Evening Post, *is considered one of the best quarterbacks in NFL history. The Hall of Famer played 17 of his 18 pro seasons with the Baltimore Colts.*

When Siblings Compete

Eli and Peyton Manning may have met in the 2006 Manning Bowl, but technically they did not actually play against each other because they were never on the field at the same time. Since both play on offense, the only time the Mannings actually made contact on the field was when the game was over and they met to shake hands.

Other siblings in sports have competed head-to-head. Throughout his career, former New York Giants running back Tiki Barber was tackled numerous times by his twin brother, Ronde, a cornerback for the Tampa Bay Buccaneers.

Venus and Serena Williams have played one another during some of the top tournaments in women's tennis. The first time they clashed in a major event was a semifinal match in 2000 at Wimbledon, the British tournament that is one of four major international tennis competitions that make up the Grand Slam. Venus won, but two years later Serena beat her older sister in the finals of another Grand Slam event, the French Open. Since then the sisters have faced one another numerous times.

Gymnasts Paul and Morgan Hamm have competed for the same medals at the Olympics. In 2004 Paul won an Olympic gold medal for individual competition as well as a silver for team competition, while Morgan won a silver for team competition. (Go back to page 27.)

The Williams sisters, Serena (left) and Venus, chat before facing each other on the tennis court at a 1999 tournament in Key Biscayne, Florida. Venus would win that match, but over the years Serena has often beaten her older sister.

Giants Stadium

Eli Manning's team plays its home games at the Meadowlands Sports Complex in East Rutherford, New Jersey. Built on the site of a former trash dump, Giants Stadium has been the home of the team since 1976. The New York Jets play there as well.

Before the stadium was built, the Giants played their home games at Yankee Stadium. When the famous baseball park was renovated in 1973, the Giants moved to the Yale Bowl in Connecticut and Shea Stadium, home of baseball's New York Mets. In the meantime the New Jersey Sports and Exposition Authority, an agency of the state government, erected a massive sports complex in a region of northern New Jersey known as the Meadowlands. The complex included a football stadium, a hockey and basketball arena, and a horse-racing track. The agency invited the Giants to become tenants of the new stadium. In October 1976 the team played its first home game there.

In 1984 the Jets moved out of aging Shea Stadium in New York and became tenants of Giants Stadium as well. In 2010 the Giants and Jets are slated to move into a new stadium in the Meadowlands, which will replace Giants Stadium. (Go back to page 28.) ◀◀

The Mannings and Hurricane Katrina Relief

Peyton and Eli Manning were both born and raised in New Orleans. After Hurricane Katrina devastated the city in 2005, the brothers returned to Louisiana to help in recovery efforts. They mobilized a planeload of relief supplies in Indianapolis, then flew on the plane to Baton Rouge, Louisiana, where they supervised its unloading. The load of supplies included 30,000 pounds of water, Gatorade, infant formula, diapers, and pillows.

Peyton organized the collection of supplies in Indianapolis. At first the Mannings did not want to make the trip to Louisiana, believing they would just get in the way of relief efforts. But officials from the American Red Cross urged them to make the trip, knowing it would be a morale booster to the people of Louisiana to see their favorite sons return with relief supplies. Said Peyton,

❝I talked to the Red Cross and told them I certainly didn't want to get in the way, but I wanted to do whatever I could to help. They said these people are down, so any kind of morale boost we could give would be good for them, too.**❞**

Since then, the two brothers have each made many trips back to New Orleans, organizing relief efforts and financing renewal projects. Said Peyton,

❝The whole town is like a family, so it's very much a personal issue.**❞**

(Go back to page 42.)

1976   Peyton Manning is born on March 24 in New Orleans, Louisiana.

1981   Eli Manning is born on January 3 in New Orleans, Louisiana.

1992   Cooper Manning is diagnosed with a spinal deformity, ending his football career at the University of Mississippi and prompting Peyton to consider other colleges.

1994   Peyton graduates from Isidore Newman High School and enrolls at the University of Tennessee.

1998   The Indianapolis Colts select Peyton as the top pick in the NFL draft on April 18. That fall he makes his NFL debut as the Colts' quarterback.

1999   Eli graduates from Newman and enrolls at the University of Mississippi. He sits on the bench as a redshirt in his freshman year.

2000   Eli is arrested in January for public drunkenness on the Ole Miss campus. On December 28, he takes over as quarterback for the Rebels and stages an exciting performance in the Music City Bowl against West Virginia.

2004   The San Diego Chargers select Eli as the top pick in the NFL draft on April 24. Immediately the Chargers trade him to the New York Giants.

2006   In the opening day matchup of the NFL season on September 10, Peyton quarterbacks the Colts against the Giants, led by Eli.

2007   Peyton quarterbacks the Colts in a win over the Chicago Bears in the Super Bowl on February 4.

2008   Eli quarterbacks the Giants to a win over the New England Patriots in the Super Bowl on February 3.

Peyton Manning
Career Statistics

Year	Team	G	Att	Comp	Pct	Yds	TD	Int	Rating
1998	Indianapolis	16	575	326	56.7	3,739	26	28	71.2
1999	Indianapolis	16	533	331	62.1	4,135	26	15	90.7
2000	Indianapolis	16	571	357	62.5	4,413	33	15	94.7
2001	Indianapolis	16	547	343	62.7	4,131	26	23	84.1
2002	Indianapolis	16	591	392	66.3	4,200	27	19	88.8
2003	Indianapolis	16	566	379	67.0	4,267	29	10	99.0
2004	Indianapolis	16	497	336	67.6	4,557	49	10	121.1
2005	Indianapolis	16	453	305	67.3	3,747	28	10	104.1
2006	Indianapolis	16	557	362	65.0	4,397	31	9	101.1
2007	Indianapolis	16	515	337	65.4	4,040	31	14	98.0

Awards

1992 Louisiana Class 2A High School MVP

1993 Louisiana Class 2A High School MVP; Gatorade Circle of Champions Award; Atlanta Touchdown Club Bobby Dodd Award; New Orleans Quarterback Club Player of the Year; Columbus, Ohio, Touchdown Club Offensive Player of the Year; Gatorade High School Player of the Year for Louisiana

1994 SEC Freshman of the Year

1995 All-SEC First Team; SEC Offensive Player of the Week (Tennessee vs. Arkansas; NCAA Offensive Player of the Week (Tennessee vs. Arkansas)

1996 All-SEC Second Team; AP All-America Third-Team; SEC Offensive Player of the Week (Tennessee vs. South Carolina); SEC Offensive Player of the Week (Tennessee vs. Georgia)

1997 Davey O'Brien Foundation National Quarterback Award; Johnny Unitas Foundation Golden Arm Award; Maxwell Football Club Award; Amateur Athletic Union James E. Sullivan Award; SEC Championship MVP; Citrus Bowl MVP; AP All-America First-Team; SEC Player of the Year; All-SEC First Team; SEC Player of the Week (Tennessee vs. Southern Miss)

1998 Top pick in the NFL draft; ESPY Award for Best College Player; NFL All-Rookie First Team

1999 NFL Pro Bowl; All-Pro Second Team; U.S. Junior Chamber of Commerce List of Ten Most Outstanding Young Americans

2000 NFL Pro Bowl; All-Pro Second Team

2001 Walter Payton/Indianapolis Colts NFL Man of the Year; Indianapolis Colts Ed Block Courage Award; Hudson Institute American Dream Award; *Indianapolis Business Journal* List of Top 40 Leaders Under 40 Years of Age; *Nuvo* magazine Best Professional Athlete in Indianapolis

2002 NFL Pro Bowl; *USA Weekend* Most Caring Athlete Award; Henry P. Iba Citizen Athlete Award; *Sporting News* Good Guys Award

2003 NFL Pro Bowl; co-winner NFL MVP; All-Pro First Team; *Nuvo* magazine Best Professional Athlete in Indianapolis; Maxwell Football Club Bert Bell Award; *Sporting News* Good Guys Award

2004 NFL Pro Bowl; Pro Bowl MVP; NFL MVP; ESPY Award for Best NFL Player; AP Offensive Player of the Year; All-Pro First Team; Maxwell Club Bert Bell Award; AFC Offensive Player of the Year; FedEx Express Player of the Year

2005 NFL Pro Bowl; ESPY Award for Best NFL Player; All-Pro First Team; ESPY Award for Best Record-Breaking Performance; Walter Payton NFL Man of the Year Award; Byron "Whizzer" White Humanitarian Award

2006 NFL Pro Bowl; All-Pro Second Team

2007 NFL Pro Bowl; Super Bowl MVP; ESPY Award for Best Championship Performance

Eli Manning
Career Statistics

Year	Team	G	Att	Comp	Pct	Yds	TD	Int	Rating
2004	NY Giants	9	197	95	48.2	1,043	6	9	55.4
2005	NY Giants	16	557	294	52.8	3,762	24	17	75.9
2006	NY Giants	16	552	301	57.7	3,244	24	18	77.0
2007	NY Giants	16	529	297	56.1	3,336	23	20	73.9

Awards

1998 *USA Today* High School Player of the Year in Louisiana; All-Metro MVP; ranked seventh in Super Prep Louisiana Top 38 High School Players

1999 University of Mississippi Chancellor's Honor Roll

2000   University of Mississippi Dean's Honor Roll; SEC Academic Honor Roll

2001   University of Mississippi Athletic Association Honor Roll; SEC Academic Honor Roll; Verizon District VI All-Academic First Team; Conerly Trophy for Best College Football Player in Mississippi

2002   University of Mississippi Chancellor's Honor Roll; University of Mississippi Athletic Association Honor Roll; SEC Academic Honor Roll; Verizon District VI All-Academic First Team

2003   University of Mississippi Athletic Association Honor Roll; Maxwell Football Club Award; Conerly Trophy for Best College Football Player in Mississippi; Birmingham Monday Morning Quarterback Club Award for SEC Most Valuable Back; *Clarion-Ledger* Sports Person of the Year in Mississippi; Jackson Touchdown Club Mississippi Amateur Athlete of the Year; National Scholar-Athlete for Division I-A; Johnny Unitas Foundation Golden Arm Award; Associated Press SEC Offensive Player of the Year; SEC Coaches Offensive Player of the Year

2004   Cotton Bowl Classic Offensive Player of the Game; All-America Football Foundation Colonel Earl (Red) Blaik Leadership Award; All-American Football Foundation All-America First Team; SEC Conference Player of the Year; *Memphis Commercial Appeal* SEC Player of the Year; SEC Coaches Player of the Year; Associated Press First Team All-SEC Touchdown Club of Atlanta Wally Butts Award for Southeast's Top Offensive Back

2008   Super Bowl MVP

Books and Periodicals

Chappell, Mike. "Super Natural," *Sports Illustrated for Kids*, vol. 17, no. 12, (December 2005).

Culpepper, Chuck. "Quarterback Central: From the Small Towns of Mississippi to the NFL, Mannings QB Dynasty Had Roots in a Different South," *Newsday* (July 27, 2004).

Manning, Archie, and Peyton Manning. *Manning*. New York: HarperEntertainment, 2000.

Myers, Gary. "Archie Knows That Eli Still Has a Ways to Grow," *New York Daily News* (Sept. 12, 2006).

Polzer, Tim. *Peyton Manning: Leader On and Off the Field*. Berkeley Heights, N.J.: Enslow Publishers, 2006.

Staple, Arthur. "Family Affair: Peyton and Eli Take Diverse Paths Toward the Same Goal," *Newsday* (July 23, 2006).

Worthington, J.A. *The Mannings: Football's Famous Family*. Bloomington, Minn.: Red Brick Learning, 2006.

Web Sites

http://www.peytonmanning.com

Peyton Manning's official Web site includes the quarterback's biography, his statistics, recent news articles about Peyton, and updates on the activities of his charity, the Peyback Foundation. Young football players can also download an application to attend the Manning Football Academy, the summer clinic on passing conducted by Peyton, Eli, and Archie Manning.

http://www.giants.com

Fans of the New York Giants can find information on the team and its players on the official Web site maintained by the team. The team's schedule, history, and statistics can be found at the Web site. Fans can also find news updates on the progress of the new stadium under construction for the Giants and the Jets.

http://www.colts.com

The official Web site for the Indianapolis Colts features many resources for Colts fans. Visitors can find statistics and biographies of players, as well as the team's annual schedule. By accessing the multimedia link, fans can listen to the radio broadcasts of some of the Colts' key plays.

http://www.olemiss.edu

Web site maintained by the University of Mississippi, where Eli and Archie Manning played their college football. Prospective students can learn about academic opportunities at the school. By following the link to Athletics, fans can find a history of Ole Miss football.

http://www.tennessee.edu

Fans of the University of Tennessee Volunteers football program can find news, statistics, and other information about the team as well as other sports at the university by following the Athletics link on the university's Web site. The university has also provided information on the site about the academic opportunities available at the school.

American Football Conference—one of two conferences featuring National Football League teams, composed mostly of the teams from the former American Football League, which merged with the NFL prior to the 1970 season. The other conference, composed mostly of original NFL teams, is the National Football Conference.

bonus—financial incentive, usually offered to an employee under special circumstances, such as exceptional performance.

commissioner—chief executive of the National Football League.

contract—legal agreement between two parties, usually requiring one party to provide services to the other in exchange for money.

cornerback—defensive player primarily responsible for ensuring the receiver does not catch the quarterback's passes.

down—attempt by the offense to advance 10 yards; under the rules, an offense has four downs to make 10 yards. If the team fails, it must turn the football over to the opponent.

freshman—first-year college student; in high school, a freshman is in the ninth grade.

fumble—miscue that results in the ball carrier losing possession of the ball during a play; either side may recover the fumble.

interception—pass caught by a defensive player.

kickoff—procedure that opens each half and also occurs after a score; the offense kicks the ball down the field to the opposing team.

NFL draft—annual procedure in which teams select college players; teams with the worst records from the prior season are given preference for picking the best college players.

quarterback—key player on offense, the quarterback is responsible for calling the play in the huddle, taking the snap from the center, and executing the play, usually by making a pass or handing the ball to a running back.

rookie—first-year professional athlete.

sack—tackle of the quarterback, resulting in a loss of yardage.

scholarship—financial aid provided to students to help them pay for college; scholarships based on athletic ability often cover the entire cost of college and require the student to play on the school's athletic teams.

sportswriter—journalist who is assigned specifically to write about sports.

Super Bowl—championship game of the National Football League, featuring the winners of the National Football Conference and American Football Conference.

wide receiver—player who serves as a prime target for the quarterback's passes.

page 6 "It certainly wasn't the situation . . ." Quoted in Jim Donaldson, "The AFC Championship Game—This Time, It's Manning's Time to Shine," *Providence Journal* (January 22, 2007), p. B-1.

page 9 "A lot of people . . . " Quoted in Allen Wilson, "Man, Oh Manning; Giants Deny Pats a Perfect Ending; Quarterback Sparks Historic Upset," *Buffalo News* (February 4, 2008), p. D-1.

page 10 "For a quarterback, there's . . ." Archie Manning and Peyton Manning, *Manning*. (New York: Harper-Entertainment, 2000), p. 193.

page 12 "I loved the recruiting, . . . " Manning and Manning, *Manning*, p. 232.

page 18 "I asked him . . . " Quoted in Joe Drape, "Eli Manning Inherits the Reins at Ole Miss," *New York Times* (October 19, 2001), p. S-1.

page 19 "Once we got close . . . " Quoted in "West Virginia 49, Ole Miss 38," CNN-*Sports Illustrated* (December 18, 2000). http://sportsillustrated.cnn.com/football/college/recaps/2000/12/28/wwh_mmo.

page 21 "They don't come much better . . ." Quoted in Kelly Whiteside, "QB Manning Has Mississippi Close to End of 40-Year Wait," *USA Today* (November 7, 2003), p. C-6.

page 21 "Everything about this year . . ." Quoted in Stephen Hawkins, "Manning Ends Drought; Ole Miss QB Carries Team to First January Bowl Victory Since 1970," *Harrisburg Patriot-News* (January 3, 2004), p. C-6.

page 22 "He's got good poise, . . ." Quoted in Peter King, "Arrival Time," *Sports Illustrated* 89, no. 23 (December 7, 1998), p. 106.

page 23 "We had a hard time . . ." Quoted in Paul Domowitch, "Little Goes Long Way for Titans Defense Able to Stop Colts' Big Weapons," *Philadelphia Daily News* (January 17, 2000), p. 114.

page 25 "Everybody's happy, . . ." Quoted in Michael Marot, "Peyton's Payday a Jackpot," *Albany Times-Union* (March 3, 2004), p. C-5.

page 27 "Peyton tortured me pretty good. . . ." Quoted in Kelly Whiteside, "Eli at Ease Being a Manning; Ole Miss Quarterback More Laid-Back Than Peyton, Archie," *USA Today* (October 4, 2002), p. C-3.

page 28 "I love both my sons . . ." Quoted in Michael O'Keefe, "Makin' Pa Proud: Archie Won't Pick a Fave as QB Sons Eli, Peyton Battle," *New York Daily News* (September 8, 2006), p. 8.

page 32 "I'm disappointed . . ." Quoted in John Branch, "Colts Defeat Giants in Opener, But Battle of Mannings is a Tie," *New York Times* (September 11, 2006), p. D-1.

page 33 "Oh my God . . ." Quoted in Gary Myers, "Archie Knows That Eli Still Has a Ways to Go," *New York Daily News* (September 12, 2006), p. 68.

page 36 "I threw it . . ." Quoted in John Branch, "Shoulder Pain Could Force Manning to Sit," *New York Times* (September 11, 2007), p. D-1.

page 40 "The only thing we evaluate . . ." Quoted in Ralph Vacchiano, "John Mara: Giants Sticking with Eli Manning," *New York Daily News* (November 14, 2007). http://www.nydailynews.com/sports/football/giants/2007/11/14/2007-11-14_john_mara_giants_sticking_with_eli_manni.html.

page 42 "What happened last year . . ." Quoted in Barry Wilner, "Shockers: Chargers, Giants—San Diego Holds Off Peyton Manning, Colts; Eli Manning, New York Knock Off the Cowboys," *Pittsburgh Post-Gazette* (January 14, 2008), p. C-1.

page 43 "This is where . . ." Quoted in "Peyton and Eli Become Teammates in Louisiana," *USA Today* (July 9, 2006). http://www.usatoday.com/sports/football/nfl/2006-07-09-manning-academy_x.htm.

page 44 "He is not only . . ." Quoted in "Children's Hospital Renamed After Manning," Channel 6 News (September 5, 2006). http://www.theindychannel.com/health/14051932/detail.html.

page 44 "This was the second year . . ." Quoted in Judy Burnett, "Meet Mrs. Manning," *Indianapolis Woman* (August 2006). http://www.indianapoliswoman.com/archive.asp?r=2006%5Caug%5Cmain-features%5Ccover%5Ccover-feature.txt.

page 46 "People ask me . . ." Manning and Manning, *Manning*, p. 370.

page 47 "I suppose Roman numerals . . ." Quoted in Frank Mathie, "Why Roman Numerals Show Up for the Super Bowl," ABC News (January 28, 2007). http://abclocal.go.com/wls/story?section=news/local&id=4979320.

page 48 "When I finally left . . ." Manning and Manning, *Manning*, p. 177.

page 53 "I talked to the Red Cross . . ." Quoted in Marsha Walton, "Manning Brothers Team Up for Katrina Relief," CNN (September 4, 2005). http://www.cnn.com/2005/US/09/04/mannings.relief/index.html.

page 53 "The whole town . . ." Quoted in Walton, "Manning Brothers Team Up for Katrina Relief."

Numbers in ***bold italics*** refer to captions.

Hal Marcovitz is a former daily newspaper journalist who has written more than 100 books for young readers. Among his titles are biographies of Venus and Serena Williams and Derek Jeter. He makes his home in Chalfont, Pennsylvania.

PICTURE CREDITS